Elena Andrioti (Phd) is a UK trained and Dubai based psychologist and mental health advocate. Through her work with children, families and educational institutions she has adopted the Dr Feelings nickname to normalize mental health for younger children.
As a mom of three boys, she blended her professional and personal experience to pen this book.

VISITING THE
Feelings
DOCTOR
Dr. Elena Andrioti
AUSTIN MACAULEY PUBLISHERS™
LONDON • CAMBRIDGE • NEW YORK • SHARJAH

Copyright © Dr. Elena Andrioti (2021)

ISBN - 9789948844327 - (Paperback)
ISBN - 9789948844310 - (E-book)

Application Number: MC-10-01-5125310
Age Classification: E

Printer Name: iPrint Global Ltd
Printer Address: Witchford, England

First Published (2021)
AUSTIN MACAULEY PUBLISHERS FZE
Sharjah Publishing City
P.O Box [519201]
Sharjah, UAE
www.austinmacauley.ae
+971 655 95 202

To my parents: Nicholas & Patricia,
for raising me to believe anything was possible.

To my husband: Patrick,
for pushing me to make those dreams a reality.

To my little superheroes: Nicholas, Alexander & Matteo
for you are my biggest inspiration.

For raising me to believe anything was possible.

For pushing me to make those dreams a reality.

For you are my biggest inspiration.

My Name is Luke and I just moved to a new country and started at a new school. This change has been hard on me.

My mom and dad know something is wrong but I don't know how to tell them how I have been feeling.

I have been feeling very sad and very angry lately.
I can't sleep well at night.
I can't eat the way I usually do.
I get pain in my tummy and sometimes cry too.

A
B
C
1
2
3
MILK

There are some things that make me feel sad about moving
to a new school.
Sometimes I get a little lost.
Sometimes I miss my old friends and teachers.
Sometimes I get a little lonely.
It's hard to explain what is going on in my heart.

SCHOOL

My mom thinks I need a little more time to get
used to my new school.
She also says I can go to a special doctor who can help
me understand my big feelings and teach me how to
handle those big feelings.
So I decided to call this special doctor: the feelings doctor.

Visiting the feelings doctor can help children and their parents solve some of the problems they face everyday. My parents decided that it was time for us to go and see her together.

When we got there, she spent time with my parents first so they could tell her what has been going on at home and at the new school.

After that, it was my turn to meet her.
The room was filled with toys and activities and I even
got to meet her stuffed little elephant "Mr. Cuddles".

At first, I felt a little shy...

JAN
12

But when my feelings doctor said I can pick any toy
I like and play with it however I want to, I felt a
little more comfortable.

ALPHABET
LETTERS
Aa
Bb
MATCH
THE COLORS

When I was done, we spent some more time playing
together and creating some fun activities.
Of course, Mr. Cuddles was there too.

We did some drawing and coloring.
We stacked blocks and raced cars but my
favorite part was the messy sand play!

JAN
12

My feelings doctor was so kind.
During my visit I even dressed up as a superhero and felt
strong enough to tell her everything I had been feeling
since I moved to a new country and started at a new school.
Talking about my feelings made me feel a little bit better.

My feelings doctor said that it is okay to feel sad and angry at times. She showed me the difference between "feeling" and "doing" and gave me many tools that I can use when I get these big emotions to help my sadness and anger leave my body.

Going to the feelings doctor helped me.
I now know what to do when I feel sad or angry.

I can't wait to show my mom and dad that I have
learned how to cope with my big emotions.
I also can't wait to visit the feelings doctor again
soon and see Mr. Cuddles too.